World Book's Learning Ladders

Play Sports!

WORLD
BOOK

www.worldbook.com

World Book, Inc.
180 North LaSalle Street
Suite 900
Chicago, Illinois 60601
USA

For information about other World Book publications, visit our website at **www.worldbook.com** or call **1-800-WORLDBK (967-5325)**.

For information about sales to schools and libraries, call **1-800-975-3250 (United States); 1-800-837-5365 (Canada)**.

Library of Congress Cataloging-in-Publication Data for this volume has been applied for.

World Book's Learning Ladders
ISBN 978-0-7166-7945-5 (set, hc.)

Play Sports!
ISBN 978-0-7166-7952-3 (hc.)

Also available as:
ISBN 978-0-7166-7962-2 (e-book)

Printed in China by Shenzhen Wing King Tong Paper Products Co, Ltd., Shenzhen, Guangdong
1st printing December 2017

Staff

Executive Committee
President: Jim O'Rourke
Vice President and Editor in Chief: Paul A. Kobasa
Vice President, Finance: Donald D. Keller
Vice President, Marketing: Jean Lin
Vice President, International Sales: Maksim Rutenberg
Vice President, Technology: Jason Dole
Director, Human Resources: Bev Ecker

Editorial
Director, New Print Publishing: Tom Evans
Senior Editor, New Print Publishing: Shawn Brennan
Writers: Jeff De La Rosa and Kyle W. Schultz
Director, Digital Product Content Development: Emily Kline
Manager, Indexing Services: David Pofelski
Manager, Contracts & Compliance (Rights & Permissions): Loranne K. Shields
Librarian: S. Thomas Richardson

Digital
Director, Digital Product Development: Erika Meller
Digital Product Manager: Jonathan Wills

Graphics and Design
Senior Art Director: Tom Evans
Coordinator, Design Development and Production: Brenda Tropinski
Senior Visual Communications Designer: Melanie J. Bender
Media Researcher: Rosalia Bledsoe

Manufacturing/Pre-Press
Manufacturing Manager: Anne Fritzinger
Proofreader: Nathalie Strassheim

Photographic credits: Cover: © Mny-Jhee/Shutterstock; © Dreamstime: 26; © Shutterstock: 4, 5, 6, 8, 10, 12, 14, 16, 18, 21, 22, 26, 27.

Illustrators: WORLD BOOK illustrations by Quadrum Ltd

What's inside?

This book tells you about some of the many kinds of sports that people play or watch around the world. You'll learn about sports you can play by yourself. You'll also learn about sports played by teams of people. All sports can be fun and help you be healthy.

 Baseball

Baseball is played with a bat and a ball on a field. A player called the pitcher throws the baseball, and the batter tries to hit it. A batter who hits the ball tries to run to three bases and then run to home plate. Players on the other team try to stop the base runner by throwing the ball to a base before the runner reaches it, or by catching the ball and touching the runner with it. If the runner touches all three bases and home plate without being stopped—called out—he or she scores a run!

It's a fact!

Baseball has been popular in the United States for over 100 years. It is sometimes called "the national pastime."

The **catcher**••••••••• squats behind home plate to catch the ball.

Wearing a **mitt** makes it easier for a player to catch the ball.

The **batter** tries to hit the ball out of the reach of the other team's players in the field.

A baseball field has three **bases** and a **home plate** arranged in the shape of a diamond.

A **baseball** is a small, hard, round ball.

A baseball **bat** is a long, piece of wood or metal. It is rounded at the top end.

Basketball

Basketball is played in a space called a court. This sport can be played indoors or outdoors. It is played between two teams. Players move the ball around the court by dribbling (bouncing) or passing it. They try to stop the players on the other team from scoring. Players score points by throwing the ball through a hoop and net called a basket.

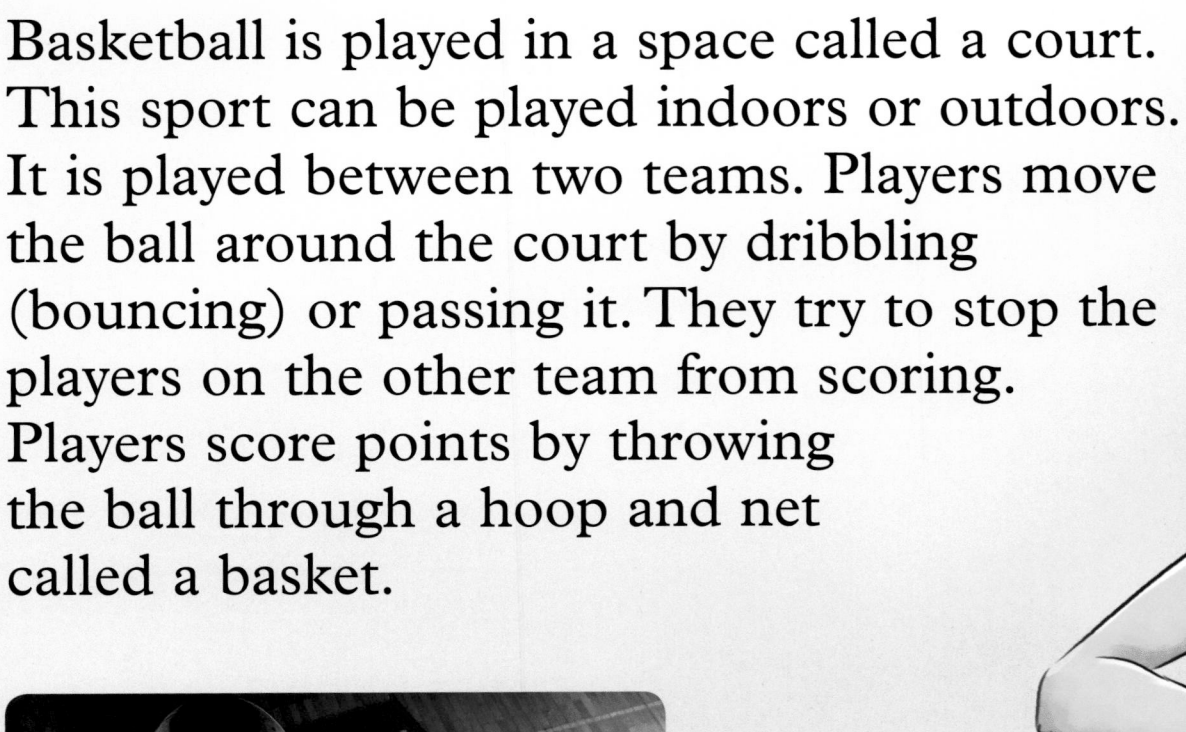

A **slam dunk** is when a player jumps and pushes the ball into the basket.

It's a fact!

The first basketball hoops were peach baskets.

The edge of the basket is attached to the **backboard**.

The ball must pass through the basket's **hoop** and **net** to score points.

The player dribbles the big, round **basketball**.

Football

American football is played by two teams on a large field. Players move the ball down the field by passing or running with it. Players on the other team try to stop the player with the ball. Players called quarterbacks hand the ball to another player on their team. After one team scores, the other team gets the ball.

Rugby is a type of football played in Australia, New Zealand, the United Kingdom, and other countries. Rugby players do not wear shoulder pads or helmets.

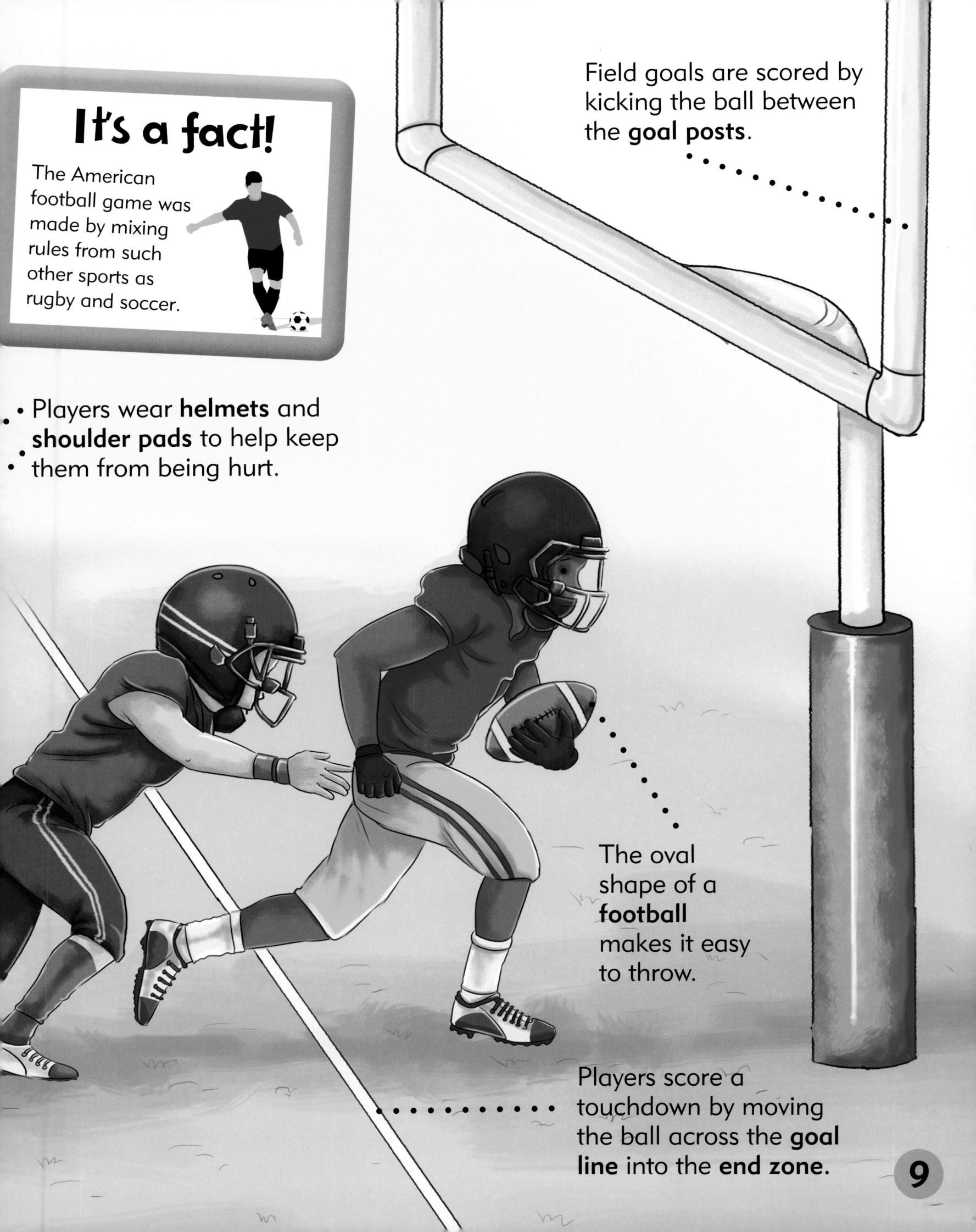

Field goals are scored by kicking the ball between the **goal posts**.

It's a fact!

The American football game was made by mixing rules from such other sports as rugby and soccer.

• Players wear **helmets** and
• **shoulder pads** to help keep
• them from being hurt.

The oval shape of a **football** makes it easy to throw.

Players score a touchdown by moving the ball across the **goal line** into the **end zone**.

9

Golf

Golf is an outdoor sport played on grass on a large piece of land called a course. Most golf courses have 18 holes in the ground. The holes are placed far apart from each other. Golfers use long sticks called clubs to hit a small ball into the holes along the course. Golfers try to get the ball into each hole using the fewest strokes (swings) of the club.

The **flag** is placed in the hole to give the golfer a target.

The **green** is the area where the hole is.

The **fairway** is the area between the tee and the green.

Golfers try to get the ball into each **hole** using the fewest strokes.

A golfer uses a **club** to hit the ball into a hole.

Play for each hole begins at a small, flat area called a **tee**.

A **golf ball** is small, white, and dimpled.

The small peg on which the ball is placed for the golfer to hit is also called a **tee**.

Hockey

The most popular kind of hockey is ice hockey. Ice hockey is played by two teams in a space called an ice rink. It is a fast-moving sport. Players use long wooden sticks to hit a small, black, round piece of hard rubber called a puck. Players pass and shoot the puck into a goal cage or net to score a goal. Players called goalies try to keep the puck out of the net.

Field hockey is another type of hockey game. It is played on the grass.

A **helmet** and thick **pads** help to keep each player from getting hurt.

Players try to shoot the puck into the **goal cage.**

Hockey players move very fast around the rink on their **skates.**

Hockey players use a wooden **stick** with a flat end to move the **puck.**

It's a fact!

Hockey pucks are frozen before hockey games to help keep them from bouncing on the ice.

Martial arts

Martial *(MAHR shuhl)* arts are sports that use fighting movements. There are many kinds of martial arts. Karate *(kuh RAH tee)*, judo *(JOO doh)*, and taekwondo *(TY kwon DOH)* are kinds of martial arts. Some groups of people have their own type of fighting styles. In most martial arts, people use their hands and feet to fight.

It's a fact!

The Japanese word *judo* means *the gentle* way. But judo competitors are often very strong and powerful!

Training takes place in a space called a **dojo**.

These martial artists fight with their **hands** and **feet**.

Capoeira *(kah poo AY rah)* is a martial art that developed in Brazil over 500 years ago. It involves back flips, cartwheels, kicks, and other big movements.

A martial artist wears a loose white uniform called a *gi* (gee).

The color of the **belt** the martial artist wears shows how good she is.

15

Snow sports

There are many sports to play in the snow! Skiing and snowboarding are outdoor winter sports that many people like. Skiers wear two long boards on their feet called skis. Skiers glide over the snow quickly. Snowboarders use one big board to slide over snow. Skiers and snowboarders can race down hills or do flying tricks. People go to special places called courses or runs to ski and snowboard.

Ski poles help skiers stay balanced.

A **snowboard** is strapped onto the snowboarder's feet.

Skiers wear **helmets** and **goggles** (covers over their eyes) to help keep them from getting hurt.

Skis attach to the skier's **boots**.

It's a fact!

Skiing straight down a hill without turning is called *schussing*.

Skis are two long boards that glide on snow.

 Soccer

Soccer is the world's most popular sport! Two teams play soccer on a field with a ball. Players—except the goalkeeper—cannot touch the ball with their hands. Players pass the ball to each other by kicking it with their feet or hitting it with their head. A goal is scored when a player kicks the ball into a net called a goal at one end of the field.

The **soccer ball** is large, light, and bouncy.

The **goalkeeper** keeps the ball out of the net. The goalkeeper can touch the ball with his or her hands.

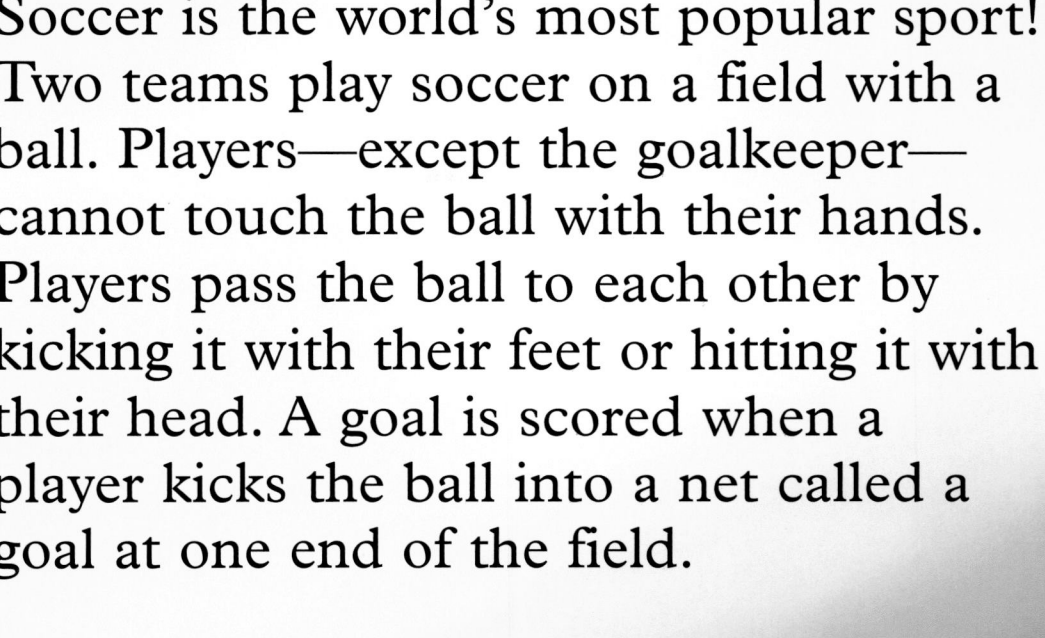

Players wear shoes with spikes called **cleats**.

Players try to kick the ball into the **goal**.

Soccer is usually played on a field of **grass**.

It's a fact!

People in most countries call soccer *football*. It is called *soccer* in Canada, Japan, and the United States. The word *soccer* comes from *assoc.*, short for *association* in Association Football.

Players use their **feet** to take the ball from a player on the other team.

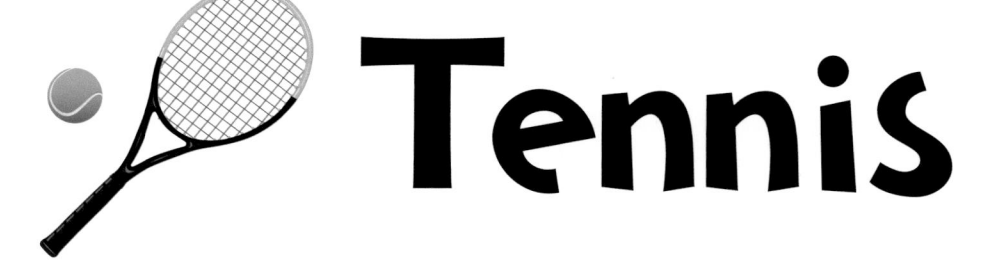

Tennis

Tennis is played with a kind of paddle called a racket and a ball. It is played in a space called a court. A net divides the court in half. Players hit a ball to one another over the net. Points are scored when a player cannot hit the ball back over the net.

It's a fact!

Tennis scores are called points, games, and sets. A score of zero is called *love*.

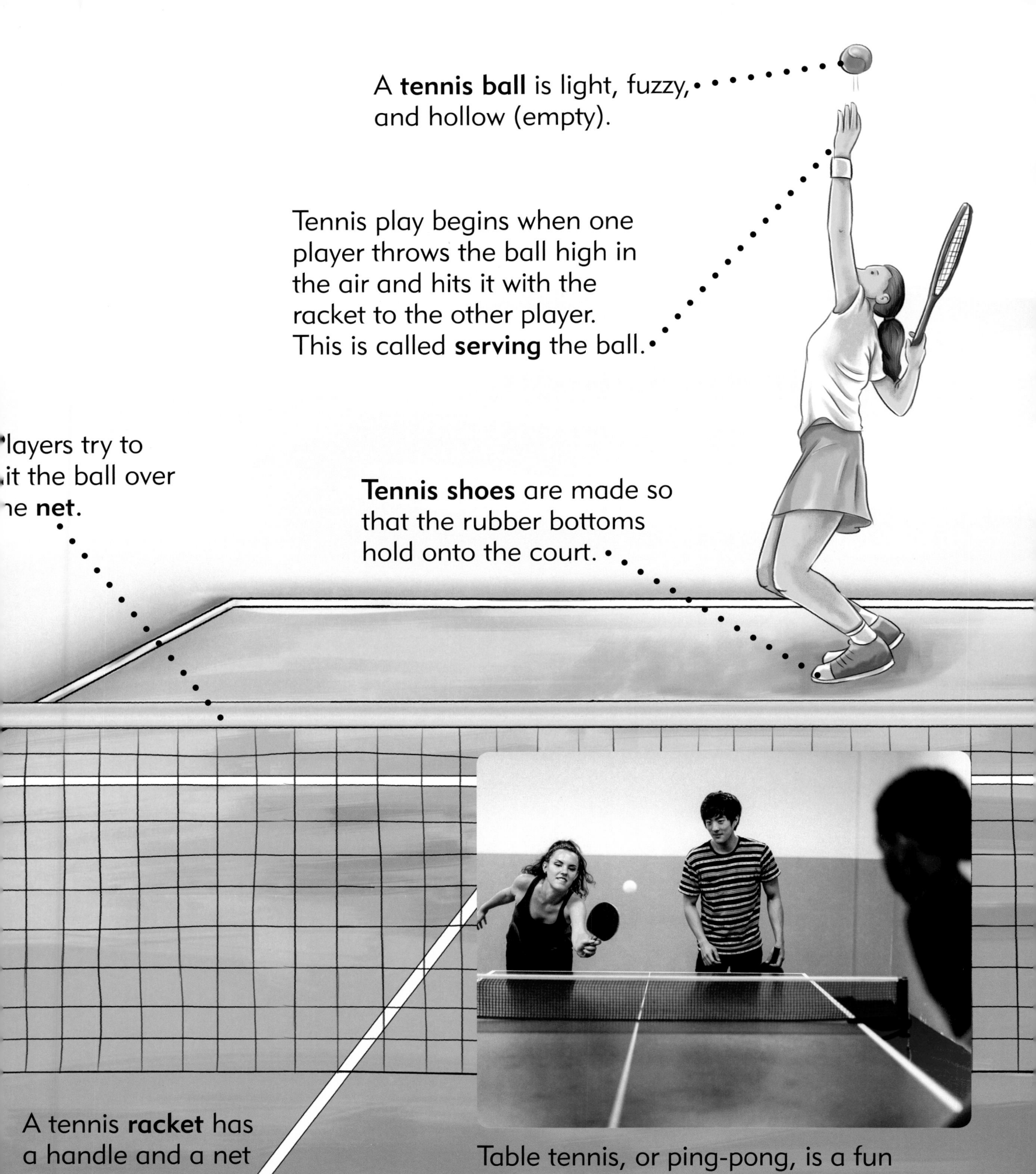

A **tennis ball** is light, fuzzy, and hollow (empty).

Tennis play begins when one player throws the ball high in the air and hits it with the racket to the other player. This is called **serving** the ball.

Players try to hit the ball over the **net**.

Tennis shoes are made so that the rubber bottoms hold onto the court.

A tennis **racket** has a handle and a net of tight strings.

Table tennis, or ping-pong, is a fun indoor game that is played like tennis.

Volleyball

Volleyball players hit a ball back and forth over a tall net with their hands, arms, or feet. A point is scored when a team cannot send the ball back over the net. Volleyball can be played indoors or outdoors. It is one of the most popular sports around the world.

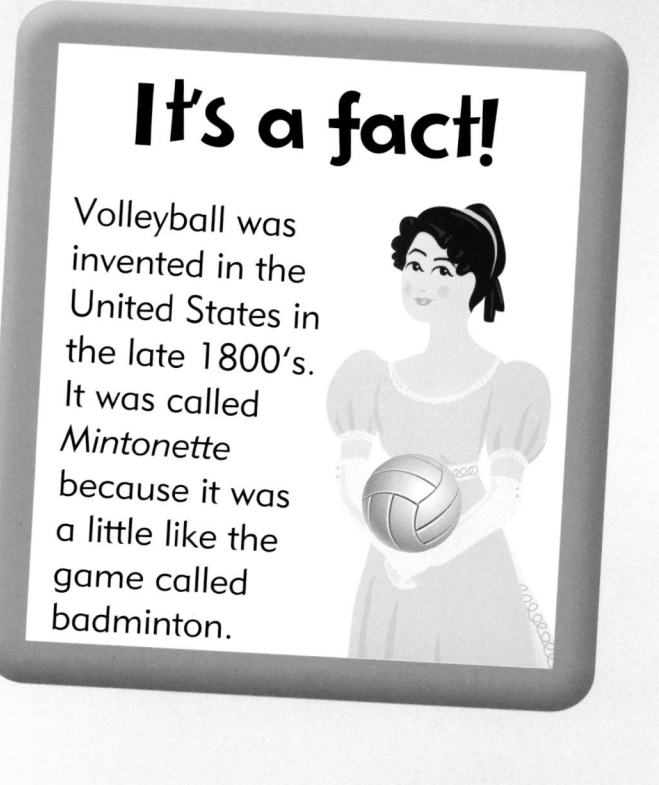

It's a fact!

Volleyball was invented in the United States in the late 1800's. It was called *Mintonette* because it was a little like the game called badminton.

Volleyball players hit a ball over a tall **net**.

Beach volleyball is played on sand. This game follows the basic rules of indoor volleyball.

Hitting the ball hard down over the net is called **spiking** the ball. • • • • • • • • •

A player cannot touch the **volleyball** two times in a row.

Indoor players wear **kneepads** for safety.

23

Play sports!

You can play many different sports right in your backyard or in a nearby park. All you need is the right kind of ball and some open space! There may be special areas set up in the park for you to use.

How many people are playing soccer?

Words you know

Here are some words that you read earlier in this book. Say them out loud, then try to find the things in the picture.

club   basketball

soccer ball   hoop

bat   mitt

25

Where is the basketball hoop?

Did you know?

Each of the Summer and Winter Olympics are held once every four years. Athletes from around the world compete in the Olympic Games.

Lacrosse is the oldest sport played in North America. It goes back to a game played by American Indian tribes hundreds of years ago.

The Special Olympics is a year-round sports program for people who have mental disabilities. It offers training and sports contests for children and adults.

More people practice karate in the United States than anywhere else in the world today.

The World Cup is a famous sporting event. It is a soccer competition that lasts for about a month.

Basketball is the world's most popular indoor sport.

Puzzles

Word jumble!

We've taken words from the book and mixed up the letters. Can you unscramble the letters to identify the words?

1. cresco

2. chokye

3. yellobvlla

4. selbbaal

5. flog

6. trimala star

Answers on page 32.

Score!

Can you match each piece of equipment above to its goal below? Follow the lines to score!

basketball   puck   football

goal cage   goal post   basket

Match up!

Match each word on the left with its picture on the right.

1. baseball bat

2. tennis racket

3. snowboard

4. volleyball net

5. gi

6. golf club

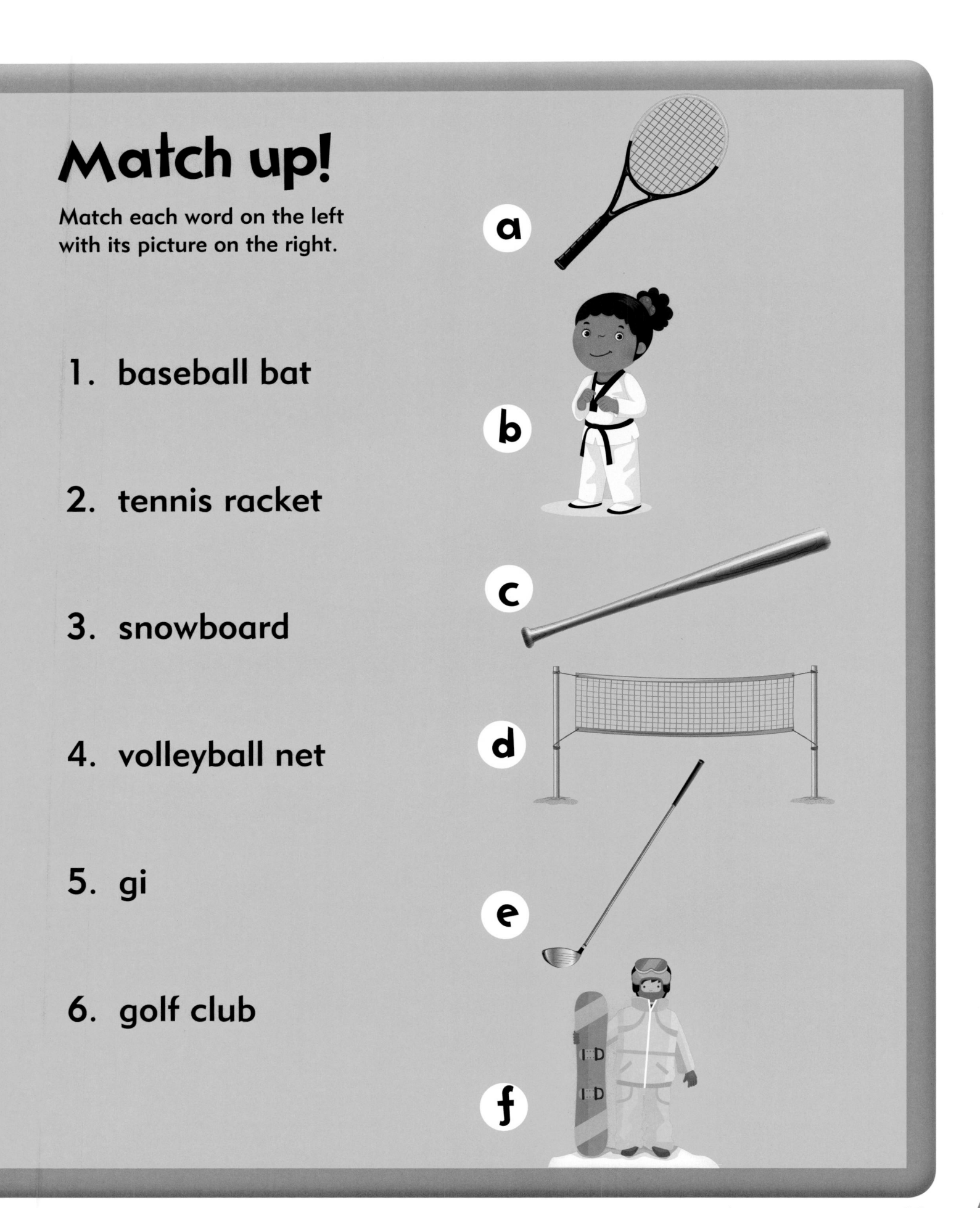

a

b

c

d

e

f

Answers on page 32.

True or false

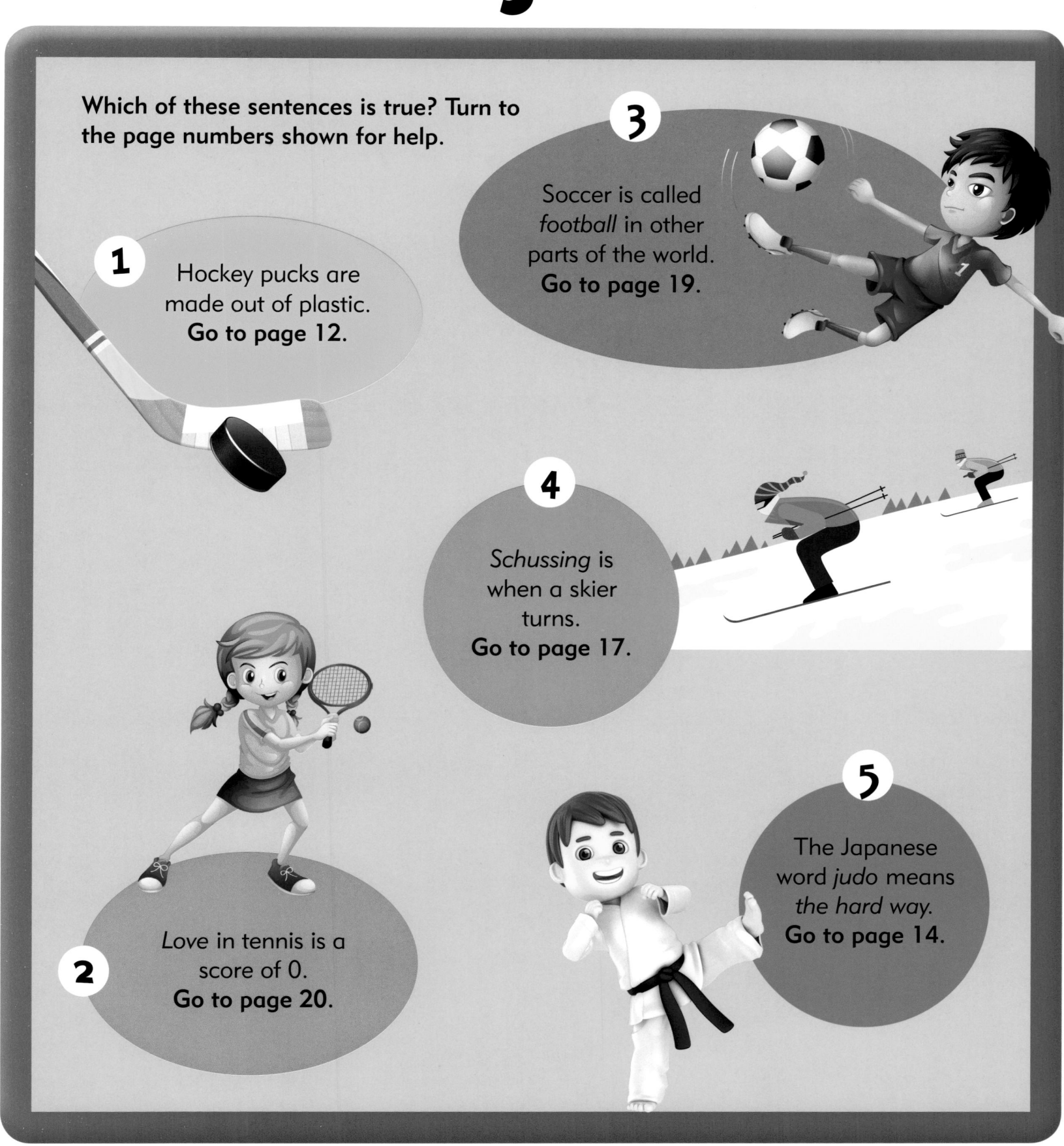

Which of these sentences is true? Turn to the page numbers shown for help.

1 Hockey pucks are made out of plastic. **Go to page 12.**

2 *Love* in tennis is a score of 0. **Go to page 20.**

3 Soccer is called *football* in other parts of the world. **Go to page 19.**

4 *Schussing* is when a skier turns. **Go to page 17.**

5 The Japanese word *judo* means *the hard way.* **Go to page 14.**

Answers on page 32.

Find out more

Books

My *First Book of Baseball* by the editors of Sports Illustrated Kids (Time Inc. Books, 2016)
This book coaches young kids through the game of baseball with a visual retelling of an actual MLB game, from the first pitch to the game-winning hit.

My *First Book of Football* by the editors of Sports Illustrated Kids (Time Inc. Books, 2015)
This lively picture book contains a solid overview of football, without the more obscure rules.

My *First Book of Hockey* by the editors of Sports Illustrated Kids (Time Inc. Books, 2016)
This illustrated book introduces the basics of professional ice hockey to children.

My *First Book of Soccer* by Beth Bugler and Mark Bechtel (Liberty Street, 2017)
This book combines informational text about soccer with action photos and two cartoon characters who add humor and give a kid's point of view.

Sporting Events: From Baseball to Skateboarding by Gabriel Kaufman (Bearport Publishing, 2006)
Discover the origins of our most popular sports.

Websites

KidsHealth
http://kidshealth.org/en/kids/
Enter the term "sports" in the search window and a list of many articles related to sports appears. Articles include "Eating for Sports," "What If I Don't Like Sports?" and "Five Ways to Avoid Sports Injuries."

Major League Baseball Kids Club
http://mlb.mlb.com/mlb/kids/index.jsp
Learn about the many leagues and programs offered to young players, get advice from experts on playing the game, and use the "Mail Call" to send a message to your favorite MLB player.

NFL Rush
http://www.nflrush.com/
The National Football League's official website has a section just for kids, featuring team scores, top news stories, games and contests, and tips on how to improve your playing skills.

Sport Science
http://www.exploratorium.edu/sports/index.html
San Francisco's Exploratorium, a science museum, has created this website to teach kids about the science behind baseball, skateboarding, bicycling, and other sports.

Answers

Puzzles
from pages 28 and 29

Word jumble!
1. soccer
2. hockey
3. volleyball
4. baseball
5. golf
6. martial arts

Match up!
1. c
2. a
3. f
4. d
5. b
6. e

True or false
from page 30

1. false
2. true
3. true
4. false
5. false

Index